McHenry Real Estate

How To Buy Sell and Invest in

Real Estate in McHenry, Illinois

Michael R. Linton, NCREA, CREIPS
Real Estate Professional

McHenry Real Estate
How To Buy Sell and Invest in Real Estate in McHenry Illinois

Copyright © 2024 by Michael Linton

All rights reserved. No part of this book may be reproduced, distributed, or transmitted in any form or by any means, including photocopying, recording, or other electronic or mechanical methods, without the prior written permission of the publisher, except in the case of brief quotations embodied in critical reviews and certain other noncommercial uses permitted by copyright law.

ISBN: 9798333953186

Published by Michael Linton

Imprint: Independently published

Cover design by Michael Linton

Interior layout and design by Michael Linton

Printed in the USA

First Edition: May 2024

For permission requests, write to the publisher at
michael@lintonglobal.com

Michael R. Linton, NCREA, CREIPS
www.McHenryAgent.com

McHenry Real Estate
How To Buy Sell and Invest in Real Estate in McHenry Illinois

This book is a work of nonfiction. Names, characters, places, and incidents are the product of the author's actual experience. Any resemblance to actual events, locales, or persons, living or dead, is entirely coincidental.

Visit our website at McHenryAgent.com

Manufactured in the USA

Printed on acid-free paper

Dedication

To my Lord and Savior, Jesus Christ,

With deep humility and reverence, I dedicate my life and my work to you. Your unwavering guidance, infinite grace, and profound wisdom have been my steadfast companions on this incredible journey. In every step and through every challenge, Your light has shone brightly, guiding me through. For Your constant and unyielding support, I am eternally grateful.

To my beloved wife and invaluable partner, Peggy Linton,

Your steadfast commitment and insightful wisdom have been the foundation of all my achievements. Your love is a ceaseless wellspring of strength and inspiration. This book stands as a heartfelt homage to the incredible partnership we share, intertwined in the deep bonds of marriage and our collaborative endeavors.

McHenry Real Estate
How To Buy Sell and Invest in Real Estate in McHenry Illinois

Table of Contents

Dedication
Table of Contents
Disclaimer
About The Author Michael Linton
Introduction
Chapter 1: Understanding the McHenry Real Estate Market
Chapter 2: Steps to Buying Your First Home in McHenry
    Assessing Your Financial Situation
    Identifying Your Home Needs and Wants
    Finding a Real Estate Agent
    Searching for Homes
    Making an Offer
    Home Inspection and Appraisal
    Closing the Deal
    Conclusion
Chapter 3: Selling Your Homes - Tips and Strategies
    Preparing Your Home for Sale
    Pricing Your Home Competitively
    Marketing Your Home Effectively
    Navigating the Selling Process
    Conclusion
Chapter 4: Investing in McHenry Real Estate: Opportunities and Strategies
    Types of Real Estate Investments

McHenry Real Estate
How To Buy Sell and Invest in Real Estate in McHenry Illinois

    Benefits of Real Estate Investing
    Risks of Real Estate Investing
    Strategies for Successful Real Estate Investing
    Conclusion

Chapter 5: Finding and Financing Investment Properties
    Identifying Investment Opportunities
    Financing Your Investment
    Evaluating Properties and Making Offers
    Conclusion

Chapter 6: Property Management and Maximizing Rental Income
    Tenant Screening and Leasing
    Maintenance and Repairs
    Rent Collection and Financial Management
    Maximizing Rental Income and Property Value
    Conclusion

Chapter 7: Legal Aspects of Real Estate Investing
    Landlord-Tenant Laws
    Real Estate Contracts
    Property Rights and Zoning
    Compliance and Risk Management
    Conclusion

Chapter 8: Tax Strategies for Real Estate Investors
    Understanding Real Estate Taxes
    Deductions and Depreciation
    Capital Gains and 1031 Exchanges
    Tax Planning Tips

Michael R. Linton, NCREA, CREIPS
www.McHenryAgent.com

Conclusion

Chapter 9: Financing Options for Real Estate Investors
    Traditional Financing Options
    Private Financing
    Hard Money Loans
    Creative Financing Strategies
    Conclusion

Chapter 10: Property Management Strategies
    Tenant Screening
    Lease Management
    Maintenance and Repairs
    Handling Tenant Issues
    Conclusion

Chapter 11: Market Analysis and Identifying Profitable Investment Opportunities in McHenry
    Understanding Market Analysis
    Conducting Market Research
    Identifying Profitable Investment Opportunities
    Conclusion

Chapter 12: Risk Management and Mitigating Potential Risks
    Common Real Estate Investment Risks
    Risk Mitigation Strategies
    Conclusion

Chapter 13: Selling Your Investment Properties
    Preparing Your Property for Sale
    Marketing Your Property
    Negotiating and Closing the Sale

Conclusion

Chapter 14: Reinvesting Your Profits and Growing Your Portfolio
      Strategies for Reinvesting Profits
      Building a Robust Real Estate Portfolio
      Conclusion

Chapter 15: Summary and Additional Resources
      Key Takeaways
      Additional Resources
      Conclusion

    Appendix: Useful Contacts and Resources
    Final Thoughts

McHenry Real Estate
How To Buy Sell and Invest in Real Estate in McHenry Illinois

Disclaimer

As a seasoned real estate broker and real estate investor with 38 years in the industry, I've garnered invaluable insights and experiences that I'm eager to share with you in this book. However, it's vitally important that I commence with a legal disclaimer. While the knowledge and strategies I present are drawn from my long-standing experience, the following pages should not be construed as providing legal, financial, or professional advice.

The realm of real estate investing is intricate and multifaceted. Each property, deal, and situation comes with its unique circumstances. While I've endeavored to deliver precise and up-to-date information, it should be seen as a general guideline or a foundation upon which to build, not as an exhaustive or personalized plan.

Even though I've done my utmost to ensure the information's accuracy at the time of writing, keep in mind that real estate markets are dynamic. Economic conditions, market trends, zoning laws, tax implications, and many other factors influencing a real estate investment can change. Given this fluidity, some details and advice might become less relevant or outdated over time.

Moreover, Chicago, like all cities, has its unique regulations and market specifics. Although many of the principles and strategies I

McHenry Real Estate
How To Buy Sell and Invest in Real Estate in McHenry Illinois

share may have broader applicability, some might be particularly relevant to the Chicagoland market and less so to other locales.

The successes I've enjoyed, which I will share with you, stem from meticulous planning, rigorous research, risk mitigation, and, at times, a little serendipity. Real estate investment involves substantial financial risk, and it is possible to lose part or all of your investment. Therefore, I implore you to seek advice from a certified professional - a lawyer, financial advisor, or real estate professional - before making significant investment decisions.

While this book discusses various investment strategies, their inclusion should not be seen as an endorsement. Each investor must assess their financial situation, risk tolerance, and investment objectives before choosing their course.

Finally, remember that real estate investing, like all worthwhile endeavors, demands dedication, patience, and continuous learning. Success rarely happens overnight; often, it's the product of consistency and resilience amid setbacks.

By proceeding with this book, you acknowledge that I - the author, broker, and investor - cannot be held liable for any decisions you make based on the information provided. You agree to accept all risks linked to real estate investments and understand it is your responsibility to conduct thorough due diligence and consult with professionals as necessary.

With that necessary preamble, I am thrilled to start this journey with you, sharing the strategies, insights, and experiences that have steered my fulfilling career in the vibrant, challenging, yet ultimately rewarding world of real estate investing

About The Author Michael Linton

Who is Michael R Linton

In the realm of real estate, experience is an invaluable asset. Michael Linton, a distinguished Broker with a prominent real estate firm, brings over 38 years of unwavering commitment and excellence in the industry. His journey is marked by not just longevity but a consistent drive to help clients achieve their real estate goals, a dedication that has earned him a reputation as a top-tier professional.

A Seasoned Real Estate Expert

Michael's illustrious career has been punctuated by exceptional achievements and a deep understanding of the real estate landscape. His expertise extends across a wide spectrum, making him a trusted advisor for both buyers and sellers. Specializing in the diverse real estate market of Chicago, Michael has honed his skills to become an adept navigator of this dynamic terrain.

With his guidance, countless clients have found their ideal properties, whether it's a charming suburban home or a bustling commercial space in the heart of the city. His clients have benefited from his in-depth market knowledge, and his extensive experience in negotiating the best deals in this competitive landscape.

Passion for Real Estate Investment

While Michael has an impressive track record in various segments of real estate, his passion shines brightest when it comes to real estate investment. He understands the unique appeal and wealth-building potential of the Chicago real estate market. Michael's expertise in investment strategies has helped numerous clients identify and secure lucrative real estate opportunities in the Windy City and its suburbs.

A Commitment to Excellence

Throughout his career, Michael Linton has been a beacon of commitment to his clients. He understands that real estate transactions are not just about properties; they are about fulfilling dreams and securing financial futures. Michael is dedicated to providing the highest level of customer service, ensuring that his clients feel valued, heard, and supported throughout their real estate journeys. His availability to address questions and concerns, paired with his personalized service, has resulted in loyal clients who return to him time and again.

A Network That Extends Locally

Michael's affiliation with a prominent real estate firm provides him with a local network that spans the entire Chicago area. With a deep understanding of the local market, Michael and his team can assist you in buying or selling a property anywhere in Chicago and its suburbs. Whether you're a first-time homebuyer or a seasoned real estate investor, Michael Linton and his team have the resources, expertise, and local insights to help you achieve your real estate goals.

A Word on Real Estate Excellence

The real estate firm Michael is associated with is renowned for its unwavering commitment to excellence. They understand that buying or selling a property is a significant life event, and their agents are dedicated to making it as smooth and stress-free as possible. With a large network of experienced agents and brokers, this firm offers comprehensive real estate services, ensuring that you receive the insights and support you need to make informed decisions.

As you embark on your real estate investment journey in Chicago, remember that you're in capable hands with

McHenry Real Estate
How To Buy Sell and Invest in Real Estate in McHenry Illinois

Michael Linton. Your aspirations for a successful real estate investment are backed by decades of experience and a commitment to your success.

Let Michael Linton and his team be your trusted guides to the world of real estate investment in Chicago. Reach out today to start your real estate investment journey. Your path to wealth and success in the Chicago real estate market awaits.

Introduction

Welcome to "McHenry Real Estate: How to Buy, Sell, and Invest in McHenry, Illinois." This book is designed to be your comprehensive guide to navigating the real estate landscape of McHenry, a vibrant community known for its picturesque surroundings and thriving property market. Whether you are a first-time homebuyer, a seasoned investor, or someone looking to sell their property, this book provides you with the knowledge and tools necessary to make informed decisions and achieve your real estate goals.

McHenry, Illinois, offers a unique blend of suburban charm and urban convenience, making it an attractive destination for families, professionals, and investors alike. The city's real estate market is diverse, featuring everything from cozy single-family homes to expansive commercial properties. Understanding this market is crucial for anyone looking to buy, sell, or invest here, and this book is structured to provide you with a step-by-step approach to mastering McHenry's real estate dynamics.

In this book, you will find detailed insights into the current state of the McHenry real estate market, including key trends, property values, and neighborhood profiles. We begin by exploring the basics of buying a home in McHenry,

McHenry Real Estate
How To Buy Sell and Invest in Real Estate in McHenry Illinois

from identifying your needs and budget to securing financing and making an offer. You'll learn about the critical aspects of home inspections and appraisals, which play a vital role in ensuring that your investment is sound.

Selling a home can be a daunting process, but with the right strategies and preparation, you can maximize your property's value and attract potential buyers. This book provides practical tips on staging your home, setting the right price, and marketing your property effectively. We also delve into the intricacies of closing the deal, helping you navigate the legal and financial aspects smoothly.

For those interested in real estate investment, McHenry presents numerous opportunities. We cover the essentials of investing in rental properties, commercial real estate, and renovation projects. You'll gain insights into evaluating potential investments, managing rental properties, and understanding the tax implications of real estate ownership.

Throughout the book, we emphasize the importance of working with qualified real estate professionals, from agents to inspectors and legal advisors. Their expertise can be invaluable in guiding you through the complexities of the real estate process, ensuring that you make informed decisions every step of the way.

McHenry Real Estate
How To Buy Sell and Invest in Real Estate in McHenry Illinois

One of the key strengths of this book is its practical approach. Each chapter is filled with actionable advice, real-life examples, and checklists to help you stay organized and focused. Whether you're looking to buy your dream home, sell your property for the best price, or build a profitable real estate portfolio, this book equips you with the knowledge and confidence to succeed.

McHenry is more than just a place to live; it's a community where you can build a future, raise a family, and achieve your financial goals. By understanding the nuances of its real estate market, you can make decisions that align with your personal and financial objectives. "McHenry Real Estate: How to Buy, Sell, and Invest in McHenry, Illinois" is your ultimate guide to making the most of the opportunities this vibrant market has to offer.

Join us on this journey through the world of McHenry real estate, and let's unlock the potential of this thriving community together.

Michael R. Linton, NCREA, CREIPS
www.McHenryAgent.com

Chapter 1: Understanding the McHenry Real Estate Market

The McHenry real estate market is a dynamic and evolving landscape that offers a myriad of opportunities for buyers, sellers, and investors. Understanding the market's unique characteristics is essential for making informed decisions and achieving your real estate goals. This chapter provides an in-depth analysis of the McHenry real estate market, exploring its history, current trends, and future prospects.

The History of McHenry Real Estate

McHenry, Illinois, located in the northeastern part of the state, has a rich history that has significantly influenced its real estate market. Originally settled in the early 19th century, McHenry has grown from a small agricultural community into a thriving suburban city. The development of transportation infrastructure, including railroads and highways, played a crucial role in its growth, making it more accessible and attractive for residents and businesses.

Over the decades, McHenry has seen various phases of real estate development, from the construction of historic homes in the downtown area to the emergence of suburban neighborhoods and commercial centers. Understanding this historical context helps in appreciating the diverse architectural styles and property types available in McHenry today.

Current Market Trends

As of recent years, the McHenry real estate market has been characterized by several key trends:

1. **Steady Population Growth**: McHenry continues to attract new residents, driven by its quality of life, excellent schools, and proximity to major employment centers. This population growth has sustained demand for housing.
2. **Diverse Housing Options**: The market offers a wide range of housing options, from historic homes in the downtown area to modern suburban developments. Buyers can find single-family homes, townhouses, condos, and apartments to suit various preferences and budgets.
3. **Rising Property Values**: Property values in McHenry have been on an upward trajectory, reflecting the area's desirability. However, the market remains relatively affordable compared to nearby urban centers, making it an attractive option for first-time homebuyers and investors.

4. **Increased Rental Demand**: The demand for rental properties has also risen, driven by a growing population and the presence of temporary residents, such as students and professionals on short-term assignments. This trend presents opportunities for real estate investors looking to enter the rental market.
5. **Commercial Real Estate Growth**: McHenry's commercial real estate sector has experienced growth, with new retail, office, and industrial developments. The city's strategic location and business-friendly environment have attracted companies and entrepreneurs, contributing to economic development.

Neighborhood Profiles

McHenry is composed of several distinct neighborhoods, each with its unique characteristics and appeal. Here are some key neighborhoods to consider:

1. **Downtown McHenry**: Known for its historic charm, downtown McHenry features a mix of residential, commercial, and recreational spaces. It offers a vibrant atmosphere with shops, restaurants, and cultural attractions.

2. **McHenry Shores**: Located along the Fox River, McHenry Shores is a desirable neighborhood for those seeking waterfront properties and outdoor activities. The area offers scenic views, boating opportunities, and a peaceful environment.
3. **Chapel Hill**: Chapel Hill is a well-established suburban neighborhood known for its family-friendly environment and excellent schools. It features a mix of single-family homes and townhouses.
4. **Boone Creek**: Boone Creek is a newer development that offers modern amenities and a suburban lifestyle. The neighborhood is known for its well-designed homes, parks, and community events.
5. **Legend Lakes**: Legend Lakes is a master-planned community that offers a range of housing options, including single-family homes and townhouses. It features parks, walking trails, and community facilities.

Market Analysis and Future Prospects

Analyzing the current market conditions and future prospects is crucial for making informed real estate decisions. Several factors influence the McHenry real estate market:

1. **Economic Indicators**: Monitoring economic indicators such as employment rates, income levels,

and consumer confidence provides insights into the market's health and potential growth.

providing you with the knowledge and tools to achieve your re**Interest Rates**: Interest rates significantly impact affordability and demand for real estate. Keeping an eye on interest rate trends helps buyers and investors plan their financing strategies.

2. **Housing Inventory**: The availability of housing inventory affects market dynamics. A balanced market with sufficient supply and demand promotes stability, while a shortage of inventory can drive up prices.
3. **Development Plans**: Future development plans and infrastructure projects can influence property values and market trends. Staying informed about upcoming projects in McHenry helps identify potential opportunities and risks.
4. **Demographic Trends**: Understanding demographic trends, such as population growth, age distribution, and household composition, provides valuable insights into the types of properties in demand and the preferences of potential buyers and renters.

Conclusion

McHenry Real Estate
How To Buy Sell and Invest in Real Estate in McHenry Illinois

The McHenry real estate market offers a wealth of opportunities for buyers, sellers, and investors. By understanding its history, current trends, and neighborhood profiles, you can make informed decisions and maximize your success in this dynamic market. In the following chapters, we will delve deeper into the practical aspects of buying, selling, and investing in McHenry real estate, providing you with the knowledge and tools to achieve your real estate goals.

Chapter 2: Steps to Buying Your First Home in McHenry

Buying your first home is an exciting and significant milestone, but it can also be a complex and daunting process. This chapter is designed to guide you through the essential steps to buying your first home in McHenry, ensuring that you are well-prepared and confident in your journey to homeownership.

Assessing Your Financial Situation

Before embarking on the homebuying journey, it's crucial to assess your financial situation and determine how much you can afford. Here are the key steps to take:

1. **Evaluate Your Savings**: Determine how much you have saved for a down payment and other associated costs, such as closing fees, moving expenses, and home inspections. A larger down payment can lower yourmonthly mortgage payments and may help you secure a better interest rate.
2. **Check Your Credit Score**: Your credit score plays a significant role in your ability to qualify for a mortgage and the interest rate you'll receive. Obtain a copy of your credit report and address any discrepancies or

areas that need improvement. Aim for a credit score of at least 620, but the higher, the better.
3. **Create a Budget**: Outline your monthly income and expenses to understand how much you can comfortably allocate toward housing costs. Include all sources of income and essential expenses, such as utilities, groceries, transportation, and existing debt payments. This will help you determine a realistic budget for your new home.
4. **Get Pre-Approved for a Mortgage**: Contact multiple lenders to get pre-approved for a mortgage. A pre-approval letter shows sellers that you are a serious buyer and provides a clear picture of your borrowing capacity. Compare different loan options and interest rates to find the best deal.

Identifying Your Home Needs and Wants

Once you have a clear understanding of your financial situation, it's time to define your home needs and wants. Consider the following factors:

1. **Location**: Decide on the neighborhoods or areas in McHenry where you would like to live. Consider proximity to work, schools, public transportation, amenities, and lifestyle preferences.

2. **Home Type**: Determine the type of home that best suits your needs, such as a single-family home, townhouse, condo, or multi-family property. Each type has its advantages and disadvantages in terms of maintenance, privacy, and cost.
3. **Size and Layout**: Consider the number of bedrooms and bathrooms you need, as well as the overall square footage and layout of the home. Think about your current and future needs, such as family size, home office space, and storage requirements.
4. **Features and Amenities**: Make a list of must-have features and amenities, such as a backyard, garage, updated kitchen, or energy-efficient appliances. Prioritize these features to help narrow down your search.

Finding a Real Estate Agent

A qualified real estate agent can be an invaluable resource in your homebuying journey. Here are some tips for finding the right agent:

1. **Research and Referrals**: Ask friends, family, and colleagues for recommendations. Research local agents online and read reviews from previous clients. Look for agents with experience in the McHenry market and a proven track record of success.

2. **Interview Multiple Agents**: Schedule interviews with several agents to discuss your needs and assess their expertise. Ask about their experience, knowledge of the local market, communication style, and availability.
3. **Check Credentials**: Verify that the agent is licensed and in good standing with the Illinois Department of Financial and Professional Regulation (IDFPR). Membership in professional organizations, such as the National Association of Realtors (NAR), can also be a positive indicator.
4. **Evaluate Compatibility**: Choose an agent with whom you feel comfortable and confident. A good agent should be attentive, responsive, and genuinely interested in helping you achieve your homebuying goals.

Searching for Homes

With your financial preparation and agent in place, you can begin the exciting process of searching for homes. Here are some tips to guide you:

1. **Use Online Tools**: Take advantage of online real estate platforms, such as Zillow, Realtor.com, and the Multiple Listing Service (MLS), to browse available

properties. Set up alerts for new listings that match your criteria.
2. **Attend Open Houses**: Visit open houses to get a firsthand look at properties and gain a better understanding of the market. This can also help you refine your preferences and identify what you like and dislike in a home.
3. **Visit Neighborhoods**: Spend time exploring the neighborhoods you're interested in. Drive or walk around to get a feel for the area, and visit local amenities, such as parks, schools, and shopping centers.
4. **Keep an Open Mind**: Be open to viewing a variety of properties, even those that may not meet all your criteria. Sometimes, a home with potential may require minor renovations or adjustments to become your dream home.

Making an Offer

Once you've found a home that meets your needs, it's time to make an offer. Here are the steps to follow:

1. **Determine Your Offer Price**: Work with your real estate agent to determine a fair and competitive offer price based on comparable properties (comps) in the

area, the home's condition, and current market conditions.
2. **Prepare the Offer**: Your agent will help you prepare a written offer, which includes the offer price, contingencies (such as financing and inspection), and the proposed closing date. Be prepared to provide an earnest money deposit, which shows your commitment to the purchase.
3. **Negotiate**: The seller may accept, reject, or counter your offer. Be prepared for negotiations and work closely with your agent to respond promptly and strategically. Stay flexible and consider compromises that are within your budget and aligned with your priorities.
4. **Acceptance and Contract**: Once your offer is accepted, you'll enter into a purchase agreement with the seller. Review the contract carefully and ensure that all terms and contingencies are clearly outlined.

Home Inspection and Appraisal

A home inspection and appraisal are critical steps in the homebuying process. Here's what to expect:

1. **Home Inspection**: Hire a professional home inspector to thoroughly examine the property's condition, including the foundation, roof, plumbing,

electrical systems, and overall structure. The inspection report will identify any issues that need to be addressed.
2. **Negotiating Repairs**: If the inspection reveals significant problems, you can negotiate with the seller to make repairs, provide a credit, or reduce the purchase price. Your agent will help you navigate this process and reach an agreement that protects your interests.
3. **Appraisal**: Your lender will require an appraisal to determine the property's market value. This ensures that the loan amount is justified and protects the lender's investment. If the appraisal comes in lower than the purchase price, you may need to renegotiate or cover the difference.

Closing the Deal

The final step in the homebuying process is closing the deal. Here's what to expect:

1. **Final Walkthrough**: Conduct a final walkthrough of the property to ensure that it is in the agreed-upon condition and that any requested repairs have been completed.
2. **Review Closing Documents**: Review all closing documents carefully, including the loan agreement,

title insurance, and settlement statement. Your agent and attorney (if applicable) will help you understand the terms and ensure that everything is in order.
3. **Closing Costs**: Be prepared to pay closing costs, which typically include fees for the loan, title insurance, property taxes, and other related expenses. Your lender will provide a detailed breakdown of these costs.
4. **Sign Documents**: Sign all necessary documents to finalize the purchase. This typically takes place at a title company or attorney's office.
5. **Receive Keys**: Once all documents are signed and funds are transferred, you'll receive the keys to your new home. Congratulations—you're now a homeowner!

Conclusion

Buying your first home in McHenry is a significant and rewarding achievement. By following these steps and working closely with your real estate agent, you can navigate the process with confidence and make informed decisions. In the next chapter, we will explore the strategies and tips for selling your home, ensuring that you can maximize its value and attract potential buyers.

Chapter 3: Selling Your Homes - Tips and Strategies

Selling your home can be both an exciting and challenging experience. The goal is to sell your property quickly and for the best possible price. This chapter provides practical tips and strategies to help you prepare your home for sale, market it effectively, and navigate the selling process smoothly.

Preparing Your Home for Sale

First impressions matter when selling your home. Proper preparation can make a significant difference in attracting potential buyers and securing a favorable offer. Here are some key steps to prepare your home for sale:

1. **Declutter and Depersonalize**: Remove personal items, family photos, and excess clutter to create a clean and neutral space. This allows buyers to envision themselves living in the home.
2. **Deep Clean**: Thoroughly clean your home, including carpets, windows, floors, and appliances. A spotless home appears well-maintained and inviting.
3. **Make Necessary Repairs**: Address any visible repairs, such as leaky faucets, cracked tiles, or

peeling paint. Small fixes can make a big difference in the overall impression of your home.
4. **Enhance Curb Appeal**: The exterior of your home is the first thing buyers see. Ensure that the lawn is mowed, bushes are trimmed, and the front entrance is welcoming. Consider adding potted plants or flowers to enhance curb appeal.
5. **Stage Your Home**: Staging involves arranging furniture and decor to highlight your home's best features and create a welcoming atmosphere. You can hire a professional stager or use online resources for staging tips.
6. **Neutralize Decor**: Use neutral colors and simple decor to appeal to a broader audience. Avoid bold or unusual color schemes that may not suit everyone's taste.
7. **Maximize Lighting**: Ensure that your home is well-lit by opening curtains, cleaning windows, and adding additional lighting if necessary. Bright and airy spaces are more attractive to buyers.

Pricing Your Home Competitively

Setting the right price for your home is crucial for attracting buyers and achieving a successful sale. Here are some tips for pricing your home competitively:

1. **Conduct a Comparative Market Analysis (CMA)**: Your real estate agent will perform a CMA to evaluate the prices of similar homes in your area that have recently sold. This analysis helps determine a competitive and realistic price for your home.
2. **Consider Market Conditions**: Assess the current market conditions in McHenry, including supply and demand, interest rates, and economic factors. A seller market may allow for a higher asking price, while a buyer's market may require more competitive pricing.
3. **Avoid Overpricing**: Overpricing your home can lead to extended time on the market and may deter potential buyers. A home that lingers on the market can become less appealing, resulting in lower offers. Price your home realistically to attract serious buyers and generate interest.
4. **Be Open to Adjustments**: Monitor the market response to your listing. If your home isn't receiving offers or generating interest, be prepared to adjust the price accordingly. Your real estate agent can provide guidance on when and how to make price adjustments.

Marketing Your Home Effectively

Effective marketing is essential to attract potential buyers and showcase your home's best features. Here are some strategies to market your home effectively:

1. **Professional Photography**: High-quality photos are critical for online listings and marketing materials. Hire a professional photographer to capture your home in the best light, showcasing its key features and attractive angles.
2. **Virtual Tours and Videos**: Virtual tours and video walkthroughs provide an immersive experience for potential buyers, allowing them to explore your home remotely. This is especially important in today's digital age, where buyers often begin their search online.
3. **Online Listings**: List your home on major real estate websites, such as Zillow, Realtor.com, and the Multiple Listing Service (MLS). Ensure that your listing includes detailed descriptions, high-quality photos, and key information about your home and the neighborhood.
4. **Social Media**: Leverage social media platforms, such as Facebook, Instagram, and Twitter, to promote your listing. Share photos, videos, and updates about your home, and encourage friends and family to share your posts.

5. **Open Houses**: Host open houses to allow potential buyers to tour your home in person. Advertise the open house through online listings, social media, and local publications. Ensure that your home is clean, well-lit, and welcoming during the event.
6. **Print Marketing**: Use print marketing materials, such as flyers, brochures, and postcards, to reach potential buyers. Distribute these materials in your neighborhood, local businesses, and community centers.
7. **Agent Network**: Your real estate agent can leverage their network of contacts to promote your listing. This includes other agents, potential buyers, and industry professionals.

Navigating the Selling Process

Once you've attracted potential buyers, it's important to navigate the selling process smoothly. Here are the key steps:

1. **Review Offers**: Your real estate agent will present you with offers from potential buyers. Review each offer carefully, considering the offer price, contingencies, and proposed closing date. Your agent will help you evaluate the strengths and weaknesses of each offer.

2. **Negotiate Terms**: If an offer is close but not quite what you want, you can negotiate with the buyer. Common points of negotiation include the offer price, contingencies, closing date, and any requested repairs or credits. Work with your agent to develop a negotiation strategy.
3. **Accepting an Offer**: Once you accept an offer, you'll enter into a purchase agreement with the buyer. This legally binding contract outlines the terms of the sale, including the purchase price, contingencies, and closing date.
4. **Addressing Contingencies**: The buyer may have contingencies in their offer, such as a home inspection or financing contingency. Be prepared to address these contingencies promptly. This may involve making repairs, providing documentation, or allowing the buyer's lender to appraise the property.
5. **Closing the Sale**: The closing process involves signing the final documents, transferring ownership, and receiving the sale proceeds. Your real estate agent, along with a title company or attorney, will guide you through this process. Be prepared to pay closing costs, which may include agent commissions, title fees, and transfer taxes.
6. **Moving Out**: Coordinate your move with the closing date. Ensure that your home is clean and all personal

belongings are removed. Leave any agreed-upon fixtures or appliances for the new owner.

Conclusion

Selling your home in McHenry can be a rewarding experience when approached with careful preparation and strategic marketing. By following these tips and working closely with your real estate agent, you can maximize your home's value and achieve a successful sale. In the next chapter, we will explore the various investment opportunities in McHenry real estate, providing insights and strategies for both new and experienced investors.

Chapter 4: Investing in McHenry Real Estate: Opportunities and Strategies

Investing in real estate can be a lucrative way to build wealth and generate passive income. McHenry offers a range of investment opportunities, from residential properties to commercial real estate. In this chapter, we will explore the different types of real estate investments available in McHenry, the benefits and risks associated with each, and strategies for successful investing.

Types of Real Estate Investments

There are several types of real estate investments to consider, each with its own advantages and challenges. Here are the primary categories:

1. **Residential Rental Properties**: These include single-family homes, multi-family properties, and condos that are rented out to tenants. Residential rentals can provide steady income and potential appreciation over time.
2. **Commercial Properties**: Commercial real estate includes office buildings, retail spaces, industrial properties, and mixed-use developments. These

investments can offer higher returns but may also involve higher risks and management complexities.
3. **Vacation Rentals**: Short-term rental properties, such as those listed on platforms like Airbnb, can generate significant income, especially in popular tourist destinations. However, they require active management and may be subject to local regulations.
4. **Fix and Flip Properties**: This strategy involves purchasing distressed properties, renovating them, and selling them for a profit. It requires a keen eye for value and a network of reliable contractors.
5. **Real Estate Investment Trusts (REITs)**: REITs allow investors to buy shares in a professionally managed portfolio of real estate assets. This provides exposure to real estate without the need for direct property ownership or management.
6. **Land Investments**: Buying land for future development or resale can be a speculative but potentially profitable investment. Consider factors such as zoning, location, and development potential when evaluating land investments.

Benefits of Real Estate Investing

Investing in real estate offers several potential benefits, including:

1. **Passive Income**: Rental properties can generate steady cash flow, providing a source of passive income for investors.
2. **Appreciation**: Real estate can appreciate over time, leading to increased property values and potential profits upon sale.
3. **Diversification**: Real estate can diversify an investment portfolio, reducing overall risk and enhancing returns.
4. **Tax Benefits**: Real estate investors may benefit from various tax deductions, including mortgage interest, property taxes, depreciation, and maintenance expenses.
5. **Leverage**: Investors can use financing to purchase properties, allowing them to control valuable assets with relatively small initial investments.
6. **Inflation Hedge**: Real estate tends to appreciate in value over time, often outpacing inflation and preserving purchasing power.

Risks of Real Estate Investing

While real estate investing offers many benefits, it's important to be aware of the risks:

1. **Market Fluctuations**: Real estate values can fluctuate due to economic conditions, interest rates,

and local market dynamics. This can impact rental income and property values.
2. **Property Management**: Managing rental properties can be time-consuming and challenging. This includes finding and screening tenants, handling maintenance and repairs, and dealing with vacancies.
3. **Financing Risks**: Real estate investments often involve significant financing, which can be affected by changes in interest rates and lending standards.
4. **Regulatory Risks**: Real estate is subject to various regulations, including zoning laws, building codes, and tenant-landlord laws. Changes in regulations can impact the profitability of investments.
5. **Liquidity**: Real estate is a relatively illiquid asset, meaning it can take time to sell properties and access cash.

Strategies for Successful Real Estate Investing

To succeed in real estate investing, it's important to have a clear strategy and follow best practices. Here are some key strategies to consider:

1. **Conduct Thorough Research**: Before making any investment, conduct comprehensive research on the local market, property values, rental rates, and

economic conditions. Understand the demand and supply dynamics in McHenry.

2. **Set Clear Goals**: Define your investment goals, whether it's generating passive income, achieving capital appreciation, or diversifying your portfolio. Your goals will guide your investment decisions.
3. **Build a Strong Network**: Surround yourself with a team of professionals, including real estate agents, property managers, contractors, and financial advisors. A strong network can provide valuable insights and support.
4. **Perform Due Diligence**: Conduct thorough due diligence on each property, including inspections, title searches, and financial analysis. Identify potential issues and assess the property's investment potential.
5. **Diversify Your Portfolio**: Spread your investments across different types of properties and locations to reduce risk. Diversification can help protect against market fluctuations and enhance returns.
6. **Leverage Financing Wisely**: Use financing strategically to maximize returns, but avoid over-leveraging. Ensure that you have sufficient cash flow to cover mortgage payments and other expenses.
7. **Stay Informed**: Keep up-to-date with market trends, economic indicators, and regulatory changes. Staying

informed will help you make proactive and informed investment decisions.
8. **Be Patient and Persistent**: Real estate investing is a long-term endeavor that requires patience and persistence. Stay focused on your goals and be prepared to navigate challenges along the way.

Conclusion

Investing in McHenry real estate offers numerous opportunities for building wealth and generating income. By understanding the different types of investments, assessing the benefits and risks, and following proven strategies, you can make informed and successful investment decisions. In the next chapter, we will explore the process of buying investment properties, including finding deals, financing options, and managing your investments effectively.

Chapter 5: Finding and Financing Investment Properties

Investing in real estate begins with finding the right properties and securing financing. This chapter will guide you through the process of identifying lucrative investment opportunities in McHenry and exploring various financing options to support your real estate investments.

Identifying Investment Opportunities

Finding the right investment properties requires a combination of market knowledge, research, and networking. Here are key steps to identify promising investment opportunities:

1. **Market Research**: Conduct thorough research on the McHenry real estate market. Understand the trends, demand and supply dynamics, property values, and rental rates. Look for neighborhoods with strong growth potential, good schools, and amenities.
2. **Networking**: Build relationships with local real estate agents, brokers, property managers, and other investors. Attend real estate networking events and join online forums to stay connected with the community. Networking can help you uncover off-

market deals and gain insights from experienced investors.
3. **Online Listings**: Utilize online real estate platforms such as Zillow, Realtor.com, and the MLS to search for properties. Set up alerts for new listings that match your investment criteria. Pay attention to distressed properties, foreclosures, and short sales, as they may offer attractive deals.
4. **Direct Mail Campaigns**: Send direct mail to property owners in your target area, expressing your interest in purchasing properties. This approach can help you find motivated sellers who are not actively listing their properties.
5. **Driving for Dollars**: Drive through neighborhoods in McHenry to identify potential investment properties. Look for signs of distressed properties, such as overgrown lawns, boarded-up windows, or "For Sale By Owner" signs. Contact the owners to inquire about their interest in selling.
6. **Public Records**: Access public records to find properties with delinquent taxes, code violations, or foreclosure notices. These properties may present investment opportunities at a discount.
7. **Real Estate Auctions**: Attend real estate auctions to bid on foreclosed properties. Auctions can offer opportunities to purchase properties below market

value, but be prepared to conduct thorough due diligence and have financing ready.

Financing Your Investment

Securing financing is a critical aspect of real estate investing. Here are various financing options to consider:

1. **Conventional Mortgages**: Conventional mortgages are traditional loans offered by banks and mortgage lenders. They typically require a down payment of 20% and have competitive interest rates. Conventional loans are suitable for investors with good credit and stable income.
2. **FHA Loans**: The Federal Housing Administration (FHA) offers loans with lower down payment requirements (as low as 3.5%). FHA loans are available to owner-occupants, so they are ideal for house hacking—living in one unit of a multi-family property while renting out the others.
3. **VA Loans**: Veterans Affairs (VA) loans are available to eligible veterans and active-duty service members. VA loans offer 100% financing with no down payment and competitive interest rates. Like FHA loans, VA loans are suitable for owner-occupants.
4. **Hard Money Loans**: Hard money loans are short-term, high-interest loans offered by private lenders.

They are based on the property's value rather than the borrower's creditworthiness. Hard money loans are ideal for fix-and-flip projects, as they provide quick financing for distressed properties.
5. **Private Money Loans**: Private money loans are funds borrowed from private individuals, such as friends, family, or other investors. Terms are flexible and negotiated between the borrower and lender. Private money loans can be a good option for investors with established networks.
6. **Commercial Loans**: Commercial loans are used to finance multi-family, office, retail, and industrial properties. They are offered by banks and commercial lenders and typically require a higher down payment and strong financials. Commercial loans are suitable for experienced investors and larger projects.
7. **Home Equity Loans and HELOCs**: Homeowners can tap into their home equity through home equity loans or home equity lines of credit (HELOCs). These loans offer lower interest rates and can be used to finance investment properties or renovations.
8. **Seller Financing**: In seller financing, the property seller acts as the lender, allowing the buyer to make payments directly to them. This arrangement can be beneficial for buyers who may not qualify for traditional financing. Terms are negotiable and can

include a down payment, interest rate, and repayment schedule.
9. **Partnerships**: Forming partnerships with other investors can help pool resources and share risks. Partners can contribute capital, expertise, or both. Ensure that partnership agreements are clearly defined and legally documented.

Evaluating Properties and Making Offers

Once you've identified potential investment properties and secured financing, it's time to evaluate the properties and make offers. Follow these steps:

1. **Property Analysis**: Conduct a detailed analysis of each property, including its condition, location, potential rental income, and expenses. Use tools like the 1% rule (monthly rent should be at least 1% of the purchase price) and the capitalization rate (net operating income divided by purchase price) to assess the property's investment potential.
2. **Comparable Sales**: Review recent comparable sales (comps) in the area to determine the property's market value. Comps should be similar in size, condition, and location.
3. **Inspection and Due Diligence**: Hire a professional inspector to assess the property's condition. Identify

any necessary repairs or renovations and factor these costs into your investment analysis. Conduct a title search to ensure there are no liens or legal issues with the property.

4. **Offer Strategy**: Develop a strategy for making offers. Consider factors such as the property's condition, the seller's motivation, and your investment goals. Be prepared to negotiate on price, contingencies, and closing terms.
5. **Purchase Agreement**: Once your offer is accepted, work with your real estate agent or attorney to draft a purchase agreement. This legally binding document outlines the terms of the sale, including the purchase price, contingencies, and closing date.
6. **Financing and Closing**: Complete the financing process by providing the lender with necessary documentation and fulfilling any conditions. Coordinate with the title company or attorney to finalize the closing. At closing, you'll sign the final documents, pay closing costs, and take ownership of the property.

Conclusion

Finding and financing investment properties in McHenry requires careful research, strategic planning, and a strong network. By following the steps outlined in this chapter, you can identify lucrative opportunities and secure the necessary financing to support your real estate investments. In the next chapter, we will delve into property management and strategies for maximizing rental income and property value.

Chapter 6: Property Management and Maximizing Rental Income

Effective property management is essential for maintaining and maximizing the value of your real estate investments. This chapter will cover the fundamentals of property management, including tenant screening, maintenance, rent collection, and strategies for increasing rental income and property value.

Tenant Screening and Leasing

Finding reliable tenants is crucial for maintaining a steady rental income and minimizing turnover. Here are key steps for tenant screening and leasing:

1. **Marketing Your Rental**: Advertise your rental property through online listings, social media, and local publications. Highlight key features, such as location, amenities, and any recent upgrades. Include high-quality photos and a detailed description.
2. **Application Process**: Develop a comprehensive rental application that collects information on the applicant's employment, income, rental history, and references. Require potential tenants to complete the application and pay a screening fee.

3. **Background Checks**: Conduct thorough background checks on applicants, including credit reports, criminal history, and eviction records. Verify employment and income by contacting the applicant's employer and reviewing pay stubs or bank statements.
4. **Reference Checks**: Contact previous landlords to verify the applicant's rental history, including payment timeliness, property care, and any issues during the tenancy.
5. **Lease Agreement**: Draft a detailed lease agreement that outlines the terms of the tenancy, including rent amount, payment due date, security deposit, maintenance responsibilities, and any rules or regulations. Ensure that the lease complies with local landlord-tenant laws.
6. **Move-In Inspection**: Conduct a thorough move-in inspection with the tenant to document the property's condition. Take photos and have the tenant sign the inspection report to acknowledge the property's state at the beginning of the lease.

Maintenance and Repairs

Regular maintenance and prompt repairs are essential for preserving property value and keeping tenants satisfied. Follow these best practices:

1. **Preventive Maintenance**: Schedule regular maintenance tasks, such as HVAC servicing, plumbing checks, and roof inspections. Preventive maintenance can help identify and address issues before they become major problems.
2. **Prompt Repairs**: Respond quickly to tenant repair requests and address issues promptly. Timely repairs can prevent further damage and maintain tenant satisfaction.
3. **Reliable Contractors**: Establish relationships with reliable contractors and service providers for maintenance and repairs. Having a trusted network can ensure quality work and timely service.
4. **Property Inspections**: Conduct periodic property inspections to assess the condition and identify any necessary repairs. Inspections can help you stay proactive in maintaining the property.
5. **Tenant Communication**: Maintain open communication with tenants regarding maintenance and repairs. Provide clear instructions for submitting repair requests and keep tenants informed of the status and timeline for addressing issues.

Rent Collection and Financial Management

Efficient rent collection and financial management are critical for maintaining cash flow and profitability. Implement these strategies:

1. **Online Payments**: Offer online payment options for rent collection, such as direct debit, credit card, or online payment platforms. Online payments are convenient for tenants and ensure timely receipt of funds.
2. **Clear Payment Terms**: Clearly outline rent payment terms in the lease agreement, including the due date, grace period, and late fees. Enforce these terms consistently to encourage timely payments.
3. **Financial Tracking**: Use property management software or accounting tools to track rental income, expenses, and cash flow. Regularly review financial reports to monitor the property's performance.
4. **Budgeting**: Develop a budget for property expenses, including maintenance, repairs, property taxes, insurance, and management fees. Budgeting helps you plan for expenses and ensure sufficient funds for ongoing operations.
5. **Reserve Fund**: Establish a reserve fund to cover unexpected expenses, such as major repairs or vacancies. A reserve fund provides financial stability and peace of mind.

Maximizing Rental Income and Property Value

Implement strategies to increase rental income and enhance property value:

1. **Upgrades and Improvements**: Invest in property upgrades and improvements that increase rental income and attract quality tenants. Consider kitchen and bathroom renovations, energy-efficient appliances, and modern amenities.
2. **Rent Increases**: Regularly review market rents and adjust your rental rates accordingly. Ensure that rent increases comply with local laws and are communicated to tenants in advance.
3. **Tenant Retention**: Focus on tenant retention by providing excellent service, maintaining the property, and addressing tenant concerns promptly. Long-term tenants reduce turnover costs and vacancies.
4. **Additional Revenue Streams**: Explore additional revenue streams, such as offering paid parking, storage units, or laundry facilities. Additional amenities can enhance tenant satisfaction and generate extra income.
5. **Curb Appeal**: Enhance the property's curb appeal by maintaining landscaping, cleaning common areas,

and making exterior improvements. A well-maintained property attracts tenants and increases value.

6. **Energy Efficiency**: Implement energy-efficient upgrades, such as LED lighting, programmable thermostats, and weatherproofing. Energy-efficient properties can reduce utility costs and appeal to environmentally conscious tenants.

Conclusion

Effective property management and strategies for maximizing rental income are essential for successful real estate investing in McHenry. By following the guidelines outlined in this chapter, you can maintain your properties, attract quality tenants, and enhance the value of your investments. In the next chapter, we will explore the legal aspects of real estate investing, including landlord-tenant laws, contracts, and compliance.

Chapter 7: Legal Aspects of Real Estate Investing

Understanding the legal aspects of real estate investing is crucial to protect your investments and comply with local, state, and federal laws. This chapter will cover landlord-tenant laws, contracts, property rights, and compliance issues you may encounter as a real estate investor in McHenry, Illinois.

Landlord-Tenant Laws

Landlord-tenant laws govern the relationship between property owners and tenants. These laws protect the rights and responsibilities of both parties. Key aspects to consider include:

1. **Lease Agreements**: A lease agreement is a legally binding contract between the landlord and tenant. It outlines the terms of the tenancy, including rent amount, payment schedule, security deposit, maintenance responsibilities, and rules for the property. Ensure your lease agreement complies with Illinois state laws.
2. **Security Deposits**: Illinois law regulates the collection, handling, and return of security deposits.

Typically, landlords can charge a security deposit equivalent to one or two months' rent. The deposit must be returned within 45 days after the tenant vacates the property, minus any deductions for damages or unpaid rent.

3. **Eviction Procedures**: Eviction is a legal process to remove a tenant from the property for violating lease terms, such as non-payment of rent or illegal activities. In Illinois, landlords must follow specific procedures, including providing written notice and filing a lawsuit in court. Evictions without a court order are illegal.
4. **Tenant Rights**: Tenants have the right to a habitable living environment, which includes functioning utilities, safe structural conditions, and proper maintenance. Tenants also have the right to privacy, meaning landlords must provide notice before entering the property, except in emergencies.
5. **Fair Housing Laws**: Fair housing laws prohibit discrimination based on race, color, religion, sex, national origin, familial status, or disability. Ensure your tenant screening and leasing practices comply with these laws to avoid legal issues and promote equal housing opportunities.

Real Estate Contracts

Contracts are essential in real estate transactions. Understanding different types of contracts and their elements is crucial for successful deals:

1. **Purchase Agreements**: A purchase agreement is a contract between a buyer and seller outlining the terms of the property sale. Key elements include the purchase price, closing date, contingencies, and property disclosures. Ensure all terms are clearly defined to avoid disputes.
2. **Option Contracts**: An option contract gives a buyer the right, but not the obligation, to purchase a property at a specified price within a certain period. Option contracts provide flexibility for investors to secure potential deals while conducting due diligence.
3. **Assignment Contracts**: Assignment contracts allow an investor to transfer their interest in a property to another buyer. This strategy is commonly used in wholesaling, where the investor assigns the purchase contract to a third party for a fee.
4. **Lease Agreements**: As mentioned earlier, lease agreements outline the terms of the tenancy. Ensure your lease agreements are detailed, legally compliant, and signed by both parties.
5. **Property Management Agreements**: If you hire a property management company, a management

agreement outlines the terms of their services, fees, and responsibilities. Review these contracts carefully to ensure they align with your investment goals.
6. **Loan Agreements**: Loan agreements between borrowers and lenders outline the terms of financing, including the loan amount, interest rate, repayment schedule, and collateral. Ensure you understand the terms and obligations before signing.

Property Rights and Zoning

Property rights and zoning laws impact how you can use and develop your real estate investments:

1. **Property Ownership**: Understand the different types of property ownership, including sole ownership, joint tenancy, tenancy in common, and community property. Each type has implications for inheritance, taxes, and property management.
2. **Easements**: Easements grant others the right to use a portion of your property for specific purposes, such as utility access or shared driveways. Be aware of existing easements and their impact on your property's use and value.
3. **Zoning Laws**: Zoning laws regulate land use and development in specific areas. Zoning categories include residential, commercial, industrial, and

agricultural. Understand the zoning regulations for your properties to ensure compliance and explore potential development opportunities.
4. **Building Codes**: Building codes set standards for construction, safety, and habitability. Ensure your properties comply with local building codes to avoid fines and ensure tenant safety.
5. **Environmental Regulations**: Environmental laws regulate issues such as hazardous materials, pollution, and land conservation. Be aware of environmental regulations that may impact your property, especially for commercial or industrial investments.

Compliance and Risk Management

Compliance with legal requirements and risk management are essential to protect your investments:

1. **Insurance**: Obtain appropriate insurance coverage for your properties, including landlord insurance, liability insurance, and property insurance. Insurance protects against financial losses from property damage, lawsuits, and other risks.
2. **Legal Counsel**: Work with an experienced real estate attorney to review contracts, resolve disputes, and navigate complex legal issues. Legal counsel can

help you avoid costly mistakes and ensure compliance with laws.

3. **Record Keeping**: Maintain thorough records of all property transactions, lease agreements, maintenance, and tenant communications. Proper record-keeping is essential for tax purposes, legal compliance, and dispute resolution.
4. **Regulatory Compliance**: Stay informed about changes in local, state, and federal laws that impact real estate investing. Compliance with regulations, such as landlord-tenant laws, fair housing laws, and building codes, is essential to avoid legal issues and penalties.
5. **Risk Mitigation**: Implement risk mitigation strategies, such as regular property inspections, tenant screening, and preventive maintenance. Proactively addressing potential risks can prevent problems and protect your investments.

Conclusion

Navigating the legal aspects of real estate investing in McHenry is essential to protect your investments and ensure compliance with laws. By understanding landlord-tenant laws, real estate contracts, property rights, and regulatory requirements, you can minimize risks and achieve long-term success. In the next chapter, we will explore tax strategies for real estate investors, including deductions, depreciation, and tax planning.

Chapter 8: Tax Strategies for Real Estate Investors

Tax planning is a critical aspect of real estate investing, as it directly impacts your profitability and long-term success. This chapter will cover tax strategies for real estate investors, including deductions, depreciation, capital gains, and tax planning tips to maximize your after-tax returns.

Understanding Real Estate Taxes

Real estate investments are subject to various taxes, including property taxes, income taxes, and capital gains taxes. Understanding these taxes and how they apply to your investments is essential for effective tax planning:

1. **Property Taxes**: Property taxes are levied by local governments based on the assessed value of the property. Property taxes fund public services, such as schools, roads, and emergency services. Ensure you budget for property taxes and understand how they are calculated in McHenry.
2. **Income Taxes**: Rental income from investment properties is subject to federal and state income taxes. Rental income is reported on your tax return,

and you can deduct eligible expenses to reduce your taxable income.
3. **Capital Gains Taxes**: When you sell an investment property, you may be subject to capital gains taxes on the profit. Capital gains are categorized as short-term (held for one year or less) or long-term (held for more than one year), with different tax rates.

Deductions and Depreciation

Real estate investors can take advantage of various deductions and depreciation to reduce taxable income:

1. **Operating Expenses**: Deductible operating expenses include property management fees, repairs and maintenance, utilities, insurance, advertising, and legal fees. Keep detailed records of all expenses to support your deductions.
2. **Mortgage Interest**: Mortgage interest on loans used to purchase or improve rental properties is deductible. This deduction can significantly reduce your taxable income, especially in the early years of the loan when interest payments are higher.
3. **Property Depreciation**: Depreciation allows you to deduct the cost of the property over its useful life, typically 27.5 years for residential properties and 39

years for commercial properties. Depreciation is a non-cash expense that reduces your taxable income.
4. **Repairs vs. Improvements**: Differentiate between repairs (deductible in the year incurred) and improvements (capitalized and depreciated over time). Repairs maintain the property's condition, while improvements enhance its value or extend its life.
5. **Travel Expenses**: Travel expenses related to managing and maintaining your rental properties, such as mileage, lodging, and meals, are deductible. Ensure your travel expenses are directly related to your rental activities and keep detailed records.
6. **Home Office Deduction**: If you use a portion of your home exclusively for managing your real estate investments, you may qualify for a home office deduction. This deduction allows you to deduct a portion of your home-related expenses, such as mortgage interest, utilities, and insurance.

Capital Gains and 1031 Exchanges

Managing capital gains taxes is crucial when selling investment properties:

1. **Long-Term vs. Short-Term Capital Gains**: Long-term capital gains (held for more than one year) are taxed at lower rates than short-term capital gains.

Plan your property sales to take advantage of long-term capital gains tax rates.
2. **1031 Exchanges**: A 1031 exchange allows you to defer capital gains taxes by reinvesting the proceeds from the sale of an investment property into a like-kind property. To qualify, you must follow specific rules, including identifying the replacement property within 45 days and closing within 180 days.
3. **Primary Residence Exclusion**: If you convert a rental property to your primary residence and live in it for at least two years, you may qualify for the primary residence exclusion, which allows you to exclude up to $250,000 ($500,000 for married couples) of capital gains from the sale.

Tax Planning Tips

Effective tax planning can significantly impact your real estate investing success. Here are some tips to help you maximize your after-tax returns:

1. **Consult with a Tax Professional**: Work with a tax professional who specializes in real estate to develop a tax strategy tailored to your investment goals. A knowledgeable advisor can help you navigate complex tax laws and identify opportunities for savings.

2. **Keep Detailed Records**: Maintain thorough records of all income, expenses, and transactions related to your investment properties. Accurate records are essential for supporting deductions and preparing your tax returns.
3. **Plan for Capital Gains**: Strategically plan the timing of your property sales to take advantage of long-term capital gains tax rates. Consider the impact of capital gains taxes when evaluating potential property sales and reinvestments.
4. **Utilize Tax-Advantaged Accounts**: Consider using tax-advantaged accounts, such as self-directed IRAs or 401(k)s, to invest in real estate. These accounts offer tax benefits, such as tax-deferred growth or tax-free withdrawals, depending on the account type.
5. **Leverage Depreciation**: Take full advantage of depreciation deductions to reduce your taxable income. Ensure you accurately calculate depreciation for each property and consider using cost segregation studies to identify additional depreciation opportunities.
6. **Implement a 1031 Exchange**: Use 1031 exchanges to defer capital gains taxes when selling investment properties. Work with a qualified intermediary to ensure compliance with IRS rules and maximize the benefits of the exchange.

7. **Consider Passive Activity Losses**: Real estate investors may be able to offset other income with passive activity losses from rental properties. Understand the rules for passive activity losses and consult with a tax professional to determine eligibility.
8. **Review Tax Laws Annually**: Tax laws change frequently, and staying informed about updates can help you adapt your tax strategy. Regularly review changes in tax laws and regulations that may impact your real estate investments.
9. **Use LLCs for Liability Protection**: Consider holding your investment properties in a limited liability company (LLC) to protect your personal assets from liability. While LLCs do not offer tax benefits, they provide valuable liability protection and can simplify estate planning.
10. **Plan for Estate Taxes**: Real estate investments can be part of your estate planning strategy. Work with an estate planning attorney to develop a plan that minimizes estate taxes and ensures your properties are transferred according to your wishes.

Conclusion

Tax strategies play a vital role in the profitability and sustainability of your real estate investments in McHenry. By understanding the various tax implications, utilizing available deductions, and implementing strategic planning, you can maximize your after-tax returns and achieve long-term success. In the next chapter, we will explore financing options for real estate investors, including traditional loans, private financing, and creative financing strategies.

Chapter 9: Financing Options for Real Estate Investors

Securing financing is a critical step in real estate investing. This chapter will explore various financing options available to real estate investors, including traditional loans, private financing, hard money loans, and creative financing strategies.

Traditional Financing Options

Traditional financing options include loans from banks, credit unions, and other financial institutions. These loans typically offer lower interest rates and longer terms but require strong credit and financial stability:

1. **Conventional Mortgages**: Conventional mortgages are standard home loans not insured by the federal government. These loans typically require a 20% down payment and are available with fixed or adjustable interest rates. Conventional mortgages are suitable for investors with good credit and stable income.
2. **FHA Loans**: Federal Housing Administration (FHA) loans are government-insured mortgages designed for first-time homebuyers and low-to-moderate

income borrowers. FHA loans require a lower down payment (as low as 3.5%) and have more lenient credit requirements. However, FHA loans are limited to owner-occupied properties, so they are not ideal for most real estate investors.

3. **VA Loans**: Veterans Affairs (VA) loans are available to eligible veterans, active-duty service members, and their families. VA loans offer competitive interest rates, no down payment, and no private mortgage insurance (PMI). Like FHA loans, VA loans are intended for owner-occupied properties.

4. **Portfolio Loans**: Portfolio loans are offered by banks and credit unions that keep the loans in their own portfolio rather than selling them to investors. These loans offer more flexibility in terms of underwriting and approval criteria, making them suitable for investors with unique financial situations.

5. **Commercial Real Estate Loans**: Commercial real estate loans are designed for properties used for business purposes, such as office buildings, retail centers, and multifamily properties. These loans typically require a higher down payment, shorter terms, and higher interest rates than residential loans.

Private Financing

Private financing involves borrowing money from individuals or private lenders rather than traditional financial institutions. Private financing can be more flexible and faster to secure, but often comes with higher interest rates and shorter terms:

1. **Private Lenders**: Private lenders are individuals or companies that provide loans to real estate investors. These loans can be secured or unsecured and typically have higher interest rates and shorter terms than traditional loans. Private lenders can be a valuable resource for investors who need quick funding or have difficulty qualifying for traditional financing.
2. **Friends and Family**: Borrowing money from friends and family is another form of private financing. While this can be a convenient and flexible option, it is essential to formalize the arrangement with a written agreement that outlines the loan terms, interest rate, repayment schedule, and any other relevant details to avoid misunderstandings and protect relationships.
3. **Self-Directed IRAs**: Investors can use self-directed Individual Retirement Accounts (IRAs) to finance real estate investments. Self-directed IRAs allow for a broader range of investment options, including real estate. It is important to follow IRS rules and guidelines to avoid penalties and ensure compliance.

Hard Money Loans

Hard money loans are short-term, high-interest loans typically used by real estate investors for fix-and-flip projects or other short-term investment strategies. These loans are secured by the property and based on its after-repair value (ARV):

1. **Fast Approval and Funding**: Hard money loans are known for their quick approval and funding processes, often within days. This makes them ideal for investors who need to act quickly on investment opportunities.
2. **Flexible Terms**: Hard money lenders offer more flexible terms than traditional lenders, including higher loan-to-value (LTV) ratios and more lenient credit requirements. However, these loans come with higher interest rates and fees to compensate for the increased risk.
3. **Short-Term Solution**: Hard money loans are typically short-term, ranging from six months to a few years. Investors use these loans to purchase and renovate properties quickly, then sell or refinance the property to repay the loan.

Creative Financing Strategies

Creative financing strategies allow investors to structure deals in ways that minimize their upfront costs and maximize their returns. These strategies include seller financing, lease options, and partnerships:

1. **Seller Financing**: In seller financing, the property owner acts as the lender, allowing the buyer to make payments directly to the seller over time. This can be beneficial for buyers who have difficulty obtaining traditional financing or want to negotiate more favorable terms.
2. **Lease Options**: A lease option allows the investor to lease a property with the option to purchase it at a later date. This strategy provides the investor with the opportunity to control a property and generate rental income while deferring the purchase decision.
3. **Subject-To Financing**: In a subject-to financing arrangement, the buyer takes over the existing mortgage payments while the loan remains in the seller's name. This strategy allows the buyer to acquire the property without obtaining new financing, often with little or no money down.
4. **Joint Ventures and Partnerships**: Forming joint ventures or partnerships with other investors can provide additional capital, expertise, and resources for real estate investments. Partners can share the

financial burden, risk, and rewards of the investment, making it easier to undertake larger or more complex projects.

5. **Equity Sharing**: Equity sharing involves partnering with an investor who provides the capital for the down payment and repairs in exchange for a share of the property's equity. This strategy allows investors to leverage their skills and experience to acquire properties without significant upfront costs.
6. **Wraparound Mortgages**: A wraparound mortgage is a type of seller financing where the seller's existing mortgage is combined with a new loan to the buyer. The buyer makes payments to the seller, who then uses part of those payments to pay the original mortgage. This can provide flexible financing terms for both parties.

Conclusion

Financing is a crucial aspect of real estate investing, and understanding the various options available can help you secure the funds needed to grow your portfolio. Whether you choose traditional loans, private financing, hard money loans, or creative strategies, it is essential to evaluate the terms, risks, and benefits of each option to make informed decisions. In the next chapter, we will explore property management strategies to maximize the value and profitability of your real estate investments.

Chapter 10: Property Management Strategies

Effective property management is key to maximizing the value and profitability of your real estate investments. This chapter will cover essential property management strategies, including tenant screening, lease management, maintenance, and handling tenant issues.

Tenant Screening

Tenant screening is the process of evaluating prospective tenants to ensure they meet your criteria and will be reliable and responsible renters. A thorough screening process can help you avoid problem tenants and reduce vacancy rates:

1. **Rental Application**: Require all prospective tenants to complete a rental application that includes personal information, employment history, rental history, and references. Use this information to verify their identity and background.
2. **Credit Check**: Conduct a credit check to assess the applicant's financial responsibility and creditworthiness. Look for a history of on-time payments, a reasonable credit score, and manageable debt levels.

3. **Background Check**: Perform a background check to identify any criminal history or previous evictions. This helps ensure the safety and security of your property and other tenants.
4. **Income Verification**: Verify the applicant's income to ensure they can afford the rent. A common guideline is that the rent should not exceed 30% of the tenant's gross monthly income.
5. **References**: Contact the applicant's previous landlords and employers to verify their rental history and employment status. Ask about their payment history, behavior as a tenant, and any issues encountered.
6. **Interview**: Conduct an interview with the prospective tenant to get a sense of their personality, expectations, and fit for your property. This can also be an opportunity to explain your rules and policies.

Lease Management

A well-drafted lease agreement is crucial for protecting your interests and clearly outlining the terms of the tenancy. Key elements to include in your lease agreement are:

1. **Rent and Payment Terms**: Specify the rent amount, due date, and acceptable payment methods. Include

details about late fees, returned check fees, and any other charges.
2. **Security Deposit**: Outline the security deposit amount, the conditions for its use, and the process for its return. Comply with local laws regarding the handling and return of security deposits.
3. **Lease Term**: Define the lease term, including the start and end dates. Specify whether the lease will automatically renew, convert to a month-to-month agreement, or require a new lease.
4. **Maintenance and Repairs**: Clarify the responsibilities for maintenance and repairs, including what the landlord will cover and what the tenant is responsible for. Include procedures for reporting and addressing maintenance issues.
5. **Property Rules**: List any rules and regulations for the property, such as noise restrictions, pet policies, and parking rules. Ensure tenants are aware of and agree to these rules.
6. **Entry and Inspection**: Specify the conditions under which the landlord can enter the property, such as for repairs, inspections, or emergencies. Include the required notice period for non-emergency entries.
7. **Termination and Eviction**: Outline the procedures for terminating the lease, including notice

requirements for both parties and the conditions for eviction.

Maintenance and Repairs

Regular maintenance and timely repairs are essential for keeping your property in good condition and ensuring tenant satisfaction. Implement a proactive maintenance strategy to address issues before they become major problems:

1. **Routine Inspections**: Conduct regular inspections to identify and address maintenance issues. Schedule inspections at move-in, move-out, and periodically throughout the tenancy.
2. **Preventive Maintenance**: Perform preventive maintenance tasks, such as servicing HVAC systems, cleaning gutters, and inspecting roofs, to extend the life of your property and avoid costly repairs.
3. **Repair Response**: Respond promptly to tenant repair requests to maintain a safe and habitable living environment. Establish a system for tenants to report maintenance issues and track the status of repairs.
4. **Contractor Relationships**: Build relationships with reliable contractors and service providers to ensure timely and quality repairs. Obtain multiple quotes for larger projects to compare costs and services.

5. **Maintenance Budget**: Set aside a portion of your rental income for maintenance and repairs. A common guideline is to allocate 1-2% of the property's value annually for maintenance expenses.

Handling Tenant Issues

Effectively handling tenant issues is critical to maintaining a positive landlord-tenant relationship and protecting your investment. Address common issues professionally and promptly:

1. **Late Rent**: Establish a clear policy for late rent payments, including grace periods and late fees. Communicate with tenants to understand the reason for late payments and work out a solution if possible.
2. **Noise Complaints**: Address noise complaints by investigating the issue and discussing it with the tenant involved. Set clear expectations for acceptable noise levels and enforce your property rules.
3. **Lease Violations**: Handle lease violations, such as unauthorized pets or occupants, by addressing the issue with the tenant and taking appropriate action. Document all violations and communications for legal purposes.
4. **Conflict Resolution**: Resolve conflicts between tenants by mediating discussions and finding mutually

acceptable solutions. Maintain open communication and foster a respectful community environment.
5. **Evictions**: Follow legal procedures for evictions, including providing proper notice and filing the necessary paperwork. Evictions should be a last resort, used only when other solutions have been exhausted.

Conclusion

Effective property management is essential for maximizing the value and profitability of your real estate investments in McHenry. By implementing thorough tenant screening, clear lease agreements, proactive maintenance, and professional handling of tenant issues, you can ensure a positive rental experience for both you and your tenants. In the next chapter, we will discuss market analysis and how to identify profitable investment opportunities in McHenry.

Chapter 11: Market Analysis and Identifying Profitable Investment Opportunities in McHenry

Conducting a thorough market analysis is crucial for identifying profitable real estate investment opportunities. This chapter will guide you through the process of analyzing the McHenry real estate market, understanding key indicators, and finding the best investment opportunities.

Understanding Market Analysis

Market analysis involves researching and evaluating various factors that influence the real estate market. By understanding these factors, you can make informed investment decisions and identify properties with the highest potential for return on investment (ROI).

1. **Economic Indicators**: Examine the local economy, including employment rates, job growth, and major industries. A strong economy with diverse employment opportunities supports a stable real estate market and attracts renters and buyers.
2. **Population Trends**: Analyze population growth, demographics, and migration patterns. Areas with increasing populations and favorable demographics,

such as a high percentage of young professionals or families, often experience higher demand for housing.

3. **Housing Supply and Demand**: Assess the balance between housing supply and demand. High demand and limited supply typically lead to rising property values and rental rates, creating favorable conditions for investors.
4. **Rental Market Analysis**: Evaluate rental market trends, including vacancy rates, average rental prices, and rental demand. Understanding the rental market helps you set competitive rental rates and forecast potential rental income.
5. **Sales Market Trends**: Analyze recent sales data, including median home prices, price appreciation, and days on market. This information provides insights into market trends and property value appreciation potential.
6. **Neighborhood Analysis**: Research specific neighborhoods within McHenry to identify areas with strong investment potential. Consider factors such as school quality, crime rates, amenities, and transportation options.

Conducting Market Research

To conduct a comprehensive market analysis, utilize a variety of data sources and research methods:

1. **Online Resources**: Use real estate websites, such as Zillow, Realtor.com, and Redfin, to gather data on property listings, recent sales, and market trends. Government websites, such as the U.S. Census Bureau and Bureau of Labor Statistics, provide valuable economic and demographic information.
2. **Local Real Estate Agents**: Consult with local real estate agents who have in-depth knowledge of the McHenry market. They can provide insights on market conditions, neighborhood trends, and investment opportunities.
3. **Public Records**: Access public records, such as property tax assessments, zoning information, and building permits, to gather additional data on specific properties and neighborhoods.
4. **Surveys and Interviews**: Conduct surveys and interviews with local residents, property managers, and business owners to gain firsthand insights into the community and housing market.
5. **Market Reports**: Review market reports from real estate organizations, such as the National Association of Realtors (NAR) and local real estate boards. These

reports provide valuable data on market trends, economic conditions, and housing statistics.

Identifying Profitable Investment Opportunities

With a thorough understanding of the McHenry market, you can identify profitable investment opportunities. Here are some strategies to help you find the best deals:

1. **Focus on High-Growth Areas**: Invest in neighborhoods with strong population growth, economic development, and demand for housing. These areas often offer higher appreciation potential and rental demand.
2. **Look for Undervalued Properties**: Seek out properties that are priced below market value due to factors such as foreclosure, distress, or motivated sellers. These properties can provide opportunities for value-add improvements and significant ROI.
3. **Consider Property Types**: Evaluate different property types, such as single-family homes, multifamily properties, and commercial real estate. Each property type has its own advantages and potential for returns.
4. **Analyze Cash Flow Potential**: Calculate the potential cash flow of rental properties by comparing rental income to expenses, including mortgage

payments, property taxes, insurance, maintenance, and management fees. Positive cash flow is essential for a sustainable investment.

5. **Assess Value-Add Opportunities**: Identify properties that offer value-add opportunities, such as renovations, upgrades, or better management. Improving the property can increase its value and rental income, enhancing your ROI.
6. **Network with Other Investors**: Join local real estate investment groups and attend networking events to connect with other investors. Networking can provide access to off-market deals, partnerships, and valuable insights.
7. **Stay Informed**: Continuously monitor the market and stay informed about changes in economic conditions, housing trends, and local developments. Being proactive and adaptable is key to identifying and capitalizing on investment opportunities.

Conclusion

Conducting a thorough market analysis and identifying profitable investment opportunities are essential steps in successful real estate investing. By understanding the McHenry market, utilizing various research methods, and employing strategic investment approaches, you can make informed decisions and achieve your investment goals. In the next chapter, we will discuss risk management and strategies for mitigating potential risks in your real estate investments.

Chapter 12: Risk Management and Mitigating Potential Risks

Risk management is a critical component of real estate investing. This chapter will cover common risks associated with real estate investments and provide strategies for mitigating these risks to protect your investments and ensure long-term success.

Common Real Estate Investment Risks

Real estate investments come with various risks that can impact your returns and investment stability. Understanding these risks is the first step in developing effective risk management strategies:

1. **Market Risk**: Market risk involves fluctuations in property values due to changes in the economy, housing market, or local conditions. Economic downturns, oversupply of housing, and changes in demand can affect property values and rental rates.
2. **Tenant Risk**: Tenant risk includes issues related to tenant reliability, such as non-payment of rent, property damage, and lease violations. Problematic tenants can lead to financial losses and increased management efforts.

3. **Vacancy Risk**: Vacancy risk arises from periods when rental properties remain unoccupied. Extended vacancies can result in lost rental income and increased carrying costs.
4. **Maintenance and Repair Risk**: Properties require ongoing maintenance and occasional repairs. Unexpected or significant maintenance issues can result in substantial costs and impact cash flow.
5. **Financing Risk**: Financing risk involves challenges related to obtaining or refinancing loans. Changes in interest rates, lending standards, or personal financial situations can affect your ability to secure financing.
6. **Legal and Regulatory Risk**: Legal and regulatory risks include changes in laws, regulations, and zoning that can impact your investments. Compliance with local, state, and federal regulations is essential to avoid legal issues and penalties.
7. **Natural Disaster Risk**: Natural disasters, such as floods, earthquakes, and hurricanes, can cause significant property damage and financial loss. Properties in disaster-prone areas are particularly vulnerable.

Risk Mitigation Strategies

To mitigate potential risks, implement the following strategies to protect your investments and ensure long-term success:

1. **Diversify Your Portfolio**: Diversification involves spreading your investments across different property types, locations, and markets. This reduces the impact of market fluctuations and economic changes on your overall portfolio.
2. **Thorough Tenant Screening**: Conduct comprehensive tenant screening to select reliable and responsible tenants. A thorough screening process reduces tenant-related risks and improves occupancy rates.
3. **Maintain Adequate Insurance**: Obtain comprehensive insurance coverage for your properties, including liability, property, and loss of rental income insurance. Adequate insurance protects against unexpected events and financial losses.
4. **Establish a Contingency Fund**: Set aside funds for unexpected expenses, such as maintenance, repairs, and vacancies. A contingency fund provides a financial cushion to handle unforeseen costs without impacting your cash flow.
5. **Regular Property Inspections**: Conduct regular property inspections to identify and address maintenance issues before they become major

problems. Preventive maintenance helps maintain property value and tenant satisfaction.

6. **Monitor Market Conditions**: Stay informed about market trends, economic conditions, and local developments. Monitoring market conditions allows you to anticipate changes and make proactive investment decisions.
7. **Use Professional Property Management**: Consider hiring a professional property management company to handle tenant screening, maintenance, and day-to-day operations. Professional management can reduce tenant-related risks and ensure efficient property management.
8. **Leverage Fixed-Rate Financing**: Use fixed-rate loans to protect against interest rate fluctuations. Fixed-rate financing provides stable and predictable loan payments, reducing financing risk.
9. **Compliance with Laws and Regulations**: Stay informed about local, state, and federal laws and regulations that impact your investments. Ensure compliance to avoid legal issues and penalties.
10. **Invest in Disaster-Resistant Properties**: When possible, invest in properties with features that reduce the risk of damage from natural disasters. Consider building materials, location, and property design to minimize disaster-related risks.

Conclusion

Effective risk management is essential for protecting your real estate investments and ensuring long-term success. By understanding common risks and implementing strategic mitigation strategies, you can safeguard your investments and achieve your financial goals. In the next chapter, we will explore the process of selling your investment properties and strategies for maximizing your returns.

Chapter 13: Selling Your Investment Properties

Selling your investment properties is a critical step in realizing your returns and achieving your financial goals. This chapter will guide you through the process of preparing, marketing, and selling your properties to maximize your profits.

Preparing Your Property for Sale

Before listing your property for sale, take the necessary steps to ensure it is attractive to potential buyers and commands the highest possible price:

1. **Conduct a Market Analysis**: Perform a market analysis to determine the current market conditions and the optimal listing price for your property. Research comparable sales, market trends, and buyer demand to set a competitive price.
2. **Make Necessary Repairs and Upgrades**: Address any necessary repairs and consider making upgrades that enhance the property's value and appeal. Focus on cost-effective improvements that provide a high return on investment, such as fresh paint, landscaping, and modern fixtures.

3. **Stage the Property**: Staging involves arranging furniture and decor to showcase the property's best features and create a welcoming environment. Professional staging can make a significant difference in how potential buyers perceive the property and can lead to quicker sales and higher offers.
4. **Enhance Curb Appeal**: First impressions are crucial. Improve the exterior of the property by maintaining the lawn, adding plants, and ensuring the entrance is clean and inviting. Enhancing curb appeal can attract more buyers and increase the property's perceived value.
5. **Gather Important Documents**: Prepare all necessary documents related to the property, such as title deeds, maintenance records, and any warranties for recent repairs or upgrades. Having these documents readily available can streamline the selling process and build buyer confidence.

Marketing Your Property

Effective marketing is key to attracting potential buyers and achieving a successful sale. Utilize a combination of traditional and digital marketing strategies to reach a wide audience:

1. **Professional Photography**: High-quality photos are essential for making a strong impression online. Hire a professional photographer to capture the property's best features and create a visually appealing listing.
2. **Create a Compelling Listing**: Write a detailed and engaging property description that highlights the unique features and benefits of the property. Use descriptive language to paint a picture of the lifestyle the property offers.
3. **Utilize Online Platforms**: List your property on popular real estate websites, such as Zillow, Realtor.com, and Redfin. These platforms attract a large number of potential buyers and provide extensive exposure.
4. **Social Media Marketing**: Leverage social media platforms, such as Facebook, Instagram, and LinkedIn, to promote your property. Share photos, videos, and engaging content to generate interest and reach a broader audience.
5. **Email Marketing**: Use email marketing to reach out to your network of contacts, including previous clients, investors, and real estate professionals. Personalized email campaigns can effectively generate interest and leads.
6. **Virtual Tours and Videos**: Offer virtual tours and video walkthroughs of the property to provide an

immersive experience for potential buyers. Virtual tours are particularly useful for out-of-town buyers or those unable to visit in person.
7. **Open Houses and Showings**: Host open houses and private showings to give potential buyers the opportunity to view the property in person. Create a welcoming atmosphere and be prepared to answer questions and highlight the property's features.

Negotiating and Closing the Sale

Once you have attracted potential buyers, the next step is to negotiate offers and close the sale:

1. **Evaluate Offers**: Review and compare offers based on price, terms, and contingencies. Consider the financial strength of the buyer, their financing plans, and their proposed timeline for closing.
2. **Negotiate Terms**: Engage in negotiations with potential buyers to achieve the best possible terms. Be prepared to negotiate on price, closing date, and any requested repairs or concessions.
3. **Accept an Offer**: Once you have agreed on terms with a buyer, formally accept the offer and proceed with the necessary paperwork. Ensure all parties understand the terms and conditions of the sale.

4. **Complete Due Diligence**: Assist the buyer with their due diligence process, which may include inspections, appraisals, and securing financing. Address any issues that arise during this period to keep the sale on track.
5. **Prepare for Closing**: Work with your real estate agent, attorney, and title company to prepare for closing. Ensure all necessary documents are in order and that any outstanding issues are resolved.
6. **Close the Sale**: On the closing date, review and sign the final documents, transfer ownership of the property, and receive the proceeds from the sale. Celebrate the successful sale of your investment property!

Conclusion

Selling your investment properties involves careful preparation, effective marketing, and strategic negotiation. By following these steps and working with experienced professionals, you can maximize your returns and achieve a successful sale. In the next chapter, we will discuss strategies for reinvesting your profits and continuing to grow your real estate portfolio.

Chapter 14: Reinvesting Your Profits and Growing Your Portfolio

Reinvesting the profits from your property sales is essential for continuing to grow your real estate portfolio and achieving long-term financial success. This chapter will explore strategies for reinvesting your profits, diversifying your investments, and building a robust real estate portfolio.

Strategies for Reinvesting Profits

Reinvesting your profits allows you to leverage your initial investment and continue building wealth through real estate. Here are some strategies for reinvesting your profits effectively:

1. **Expand Your Portfolio**: Use the proceeds from your property sales to purchase additional investment properties. Expanding your portfolio increases your potential for rental income and property appreciation.
2. **Diversify Property Types**: Diversify your investments by acquiring different types of properties, such as residential, commercial, and industrial. Diversification reduces risk and provides multiple streams of income.

3. **Invest in Different Locations**: Consider investing in properties in various geographic locations. Diversifying your investments across different markets can mitigate the impact of local economic fluctuations.
4. **Value-Add Investments**: Look for properties with value-add opportunities, such as those that require renovations or have the potential for increased rental income. Investing in value-add properties can provide higher returns through property improvements.
5. **Real Estate Investment Trusts (REITs)**: Allocate a portion of your profits to REITs, which allow you to invest in a diversified portfolio of real estate assets without directly owning properties. REITs provide liquidity and passive income through dividends.
6. **Participate in Syndications**: Join real estate syndications or partnerships where multiple investors pool their resources to acquire larger properties or development projects. Syndications provide access to larger investment opportunities and shared risk.
7. **Short-Term Rentals**: Invest in short-term rental properties, such as vacation rentals or Airbnb listings. Short-term rentals can generate higher rental income compared to traditional long-term leases.
8. **Commercial Real Estate**: Consider investing in commercial properties, such as office buildings, retail spaces, or industrial warehouses. Commercial real

estate can provide stable cash flow and long-term leases.

Building a Robust Real Estate Portfolio

To build a robust and sustainable real estate portfolio, implement the following best practices:

1. **Set Clear Goals**: Define your investment goals, such as income generation, property appreciation, or portfolio diversification. Clear goals guide your investment decisions and strategy.
2. **Conduct Thorough Due Diligence**: Perform comprehensive due diligence on every property you consider, including market analysis, property inspections, and financial evaluations. Thorough due diligence reduces risk and ensures informed investment decisions.
3. **Maintain Financial Discipline**: Manage your finances prudently by maintaining adequate cash reserves, avoiding overleveraging, and monitoring your cash flow. Financial discipline is essential for long-term investment success.
4. **Monitor and Adjust Your Portfolio**: Regularly review your portfolio's performance and make adjustments as needed. Rebalance your investments,

address underperforming properties, and seize new opportunities.

5. **Stay Informed**: Continuously educate yourself about real estate market trends, economic conditions, and investment strategies. Staying informed helps you adapt to changing market dynamics and make informed decisions.
6. **Leverage Professional Expertise**: Work with experienced real estate professionals, such as agents, property managers, attorneys, and accountants. Professional expertise enhances your investment strategy and ensures compliance with regulations.
7. **Network with Other Investors**: Build relationships with other real estate investors through networking events, investment groups, and online forums. Networking provides valuable insights, partnerships, and access to off-market deals.
8. **Focus on Long-Term Growth**: Prioritize long-term growth over short-term gains. A patient and strategic approach to real estate investing builds lasting wealth and financial stability.

Conclusion

Reinvesting your profits and growing your real estate portfolio is a continuous process that requires strategic planning, diversification, and ongoing education. By implementing these strategies and best practices, you can achieve long-term financial success and build a robust real estate portfolio. In the final chapter, we will summarize the key takeaways from this guide and provide additional resources for your real estate investment journey.

Chapter 15: Summary and Additional Resources

In this final chapter, we will summarize the key takeaways from this guide and provide additional resources to support your real estate investment journey in McHenry, Illinois.

Key Takeaways

1. **Understanding the Market**: Conduct thorough market analysis to understand economic indicators, population trends, housing supply and demand, rental and sales market trends, and neighborhood dynamics.
2. **Financing Your Investments**: Explore various financing options, including conventional loans, FHA loans, VA loans, USDA loans, hard money loans, private money loans, and seller financing.
3. **Finding Investment Properties**: Utilize online resources, real estate agents, public records, auctions, networking, and direct marketing to find investment properties.
4. **Evaluating Properties**: Perform detailed property evaluations, including financial analysis, cash flow projections, cap rate calculations, and physical inspections.

5. **Managing Rental Properties**: Implement effective property management practices, including tenant screening, lease agreements, rent collection, maintenance, and legal compliance.
6. **Maximizing ROI**: Focus on property improvements, effective marketing, competitive rental rates, and minimizing vacancies to maximize your return on investment.
7. **Selling Investment Properties**: Prepare, market, and sell your properties strategically to achieve the highest possible returns.
8. **Risk Management**: Implement risk mitigation strategies, including diversification, tenant screening, insurance, contingency funds, and professional property management.
9. **Reinvesting Profits**: Reinvest your profits to expand your portfolio, diversify your investments, and continue building wealth through real estate.
10. **Building a Robust Portfolio**: Set clear goals, conduct due diligence, maintain financial discipline, monitor your portfolio, stay informed, leverage professional expertise, and network with other investors.

Additional Resources

o further support your real estate investment journey, consider the following resources:

1. **Books and Publications**: Read books on real estate investing to deepen your knowledge and gain insights from experienced investors. Recommended titles include:
    - "Rich Dad Poor Dad" by Robert Kiyosaki
    - "The Millionaire Real Estate Investor" by Gary Keller
    - "Investing in Apartment Buildings" by Matthew A. Martinez
    - "Real Estate Investing For Dummies" by Eric Tyson and Robert S. Griswold
2. **Online Courses and Webinars**: Enroll in online courses and webinars to learn from industry experts and stay updated on the latest trends and strategies. Platforms like Udemy, Coursera, and BiggerPockets offer a wide range of real estate investing courses.
3. **Real Estate Investment Groups**: Join local or online real estate investment groups to network with other investors, share experiences, and discover new opportunities. Websites like Meetup and BiggerPockets have active communities for real estate investors.

4. **Professional Associations**: Become a member of professional associations, such as the National Real Estate Investors Association (NREIA) and local real estate investment clubs. These organizations provide valuable resources, networking opportunities, and educational events.
5. **Real Estate Investment Blogs and Podcasts**: Follow blogs and podcasts dedicated to real estate investing to stay informed about market trends, investment strategies, and success stories. Popular blogs include BiggerPockets, REtipster, and The Real Estate Guys.
6. **Real Estate Tools and Software**: Utilize real estate tools and software to analyze properties, manage investments, and streamline your operations. Recommended tools include:
    - DealCheck for property analysis
    - Stessa for property management
    - PropStream for property data and lead generation
    - Roofstock for turnkey investment properties
7. **Consult with Real Estate Professionals**: Work with experienced real estate agents, property managers, attorneys, and accountants who specialize in real estate investments. Their expertise can help you

make informed decisions and navigate complex transactions.

8. **Attend Real Estate Conferences and Events**: Participate in real estate conferences and events to learn from industry leaders, network with other investors, and discover new investment opportunities. Notable events include the National Association of Realtors (NAR) Annual Conference and the BiggerPockets Real Estate Conference.

Conclusion

Embarking on a real estate investment journey in McHenry, Illinois, offers numerous opportunities for financial growth and success. By following the strategies outlined in this guide, conducting thorough research, and leveraging available resources, you can make informed investment decisions and build a robust real estate portfolio. Remember that real estate investing is a long-term endeavor that requires patience, discipline, and continuous learning.

We hope this guide has provided valuable insights and practical advice to support your real estate investment endeavors. Best of luck on your journey to becoming a successful real estate investor in McHenry, Illinois!

Appendix: Useful Contacts and Resources

- **McHenry County Association of Realtors**: Provides local market data, networking events, and educational resources.
- **McHenry County Government**: Access property records, zoning information, and tax assessments.
- **Illinois Department of Financial and Professional Regulation (IDFPR)**: Licensing and regulatory information for real estate professionals.
- **Local Real Estate Attorneys and Accountants**: For legal and financial advice specific to real estate investments.
- **Home Inspection Services**: For thorough property inspections and evaluations.
- **Property Management Companies**: For managing rental properties and ensuring tenant satisfaction.

By utilizing these resources and applying the knowledge gained from this guide, you can confidently navigate the real estate market in McHenry, Illinois, and achieve your investment goals.

- **Title Companies**: For ensuring clear title transfer and handling closing procedures. Some reputable title companies in McHenry include:
    - Fidelity National Title
    - Chicago Title Insurance Company
    - First American Title
- **Mortgage Brokers and Lenders**: For financing options and loan advice. Consider working with:
    - Guaranteed Rate
    - Quicken Loans

- ○ Wells Fargo Home Mortgage
- **Local Chambers of Commerce**: Join for networking opportunities and local business insights. The McHenry Area Chamber of Commerce is a valuable resource for real estate investors.
- **Local Economic Development Corporations**: For information on economic trends and development opportunities. The McHenry County Economic Development Corporation provides resources and support for investors.

Final Thoughts

Real estate investing in McHenry, Illinois, presents a unique opportunity to build wealth and secure financial independence. By adhering to the strategies and advice provided in this guide, you can navigate the complexities of the real estate market with confidence. Remember, successful investing requires diligence, patience, and a willingness to learn and adapt.

Whether you are just starting out or are an experienced investor, McHenry offers a range of opportunities that can help you achieve your financial goals. Stay informed, network with other professionals, and continue to educate yourself to stay ahead in the ever-evolving real estate market.

Thank you for reading "McHenry Real Estate: How to Buy, Sell, and Invest in McHenry, Illinois." We wish you the best of luck in

McHenry Real Estate
How To Buy Sell and Invest in Real Estate in McHenry Illinois

your real estate investment journey. May your investments be prosperous and your portfolio grow steadily.

Michael R. Linton, NCREA, CREIPS
www.McHenryAgent.com

www.ingramcontent.com/pod-product-compliance
Lightning Source LLC
Chambersburg PA
CBHW071937210526
45479CB00002B/712